Delightful task! to rear the tender thought,
To teach the young idea how to shoot,
To pour the fresh instruction o'er the mind,
To breathe th' enlivening spirit, and to fix
The generous purpose in the glowing breast.

Thomson

Note to Parents and Teachers

Poems hold a special magic for children; it's as if the poet has looked into their souls and written what they feel, hope, and wonder about.

Poetry is an effective and enjoyable means for children to learn critical reading skills as well as values which are essential to a happy and productive life.

The poems in this book were written to help children develop self-esteem and understand that they have much in common with other people. Above all, it is my fondest hope that this book will bring much joy into your home. Open these pages and come with me on a delightful visit into a child's world of fun and fantasy.

The Author

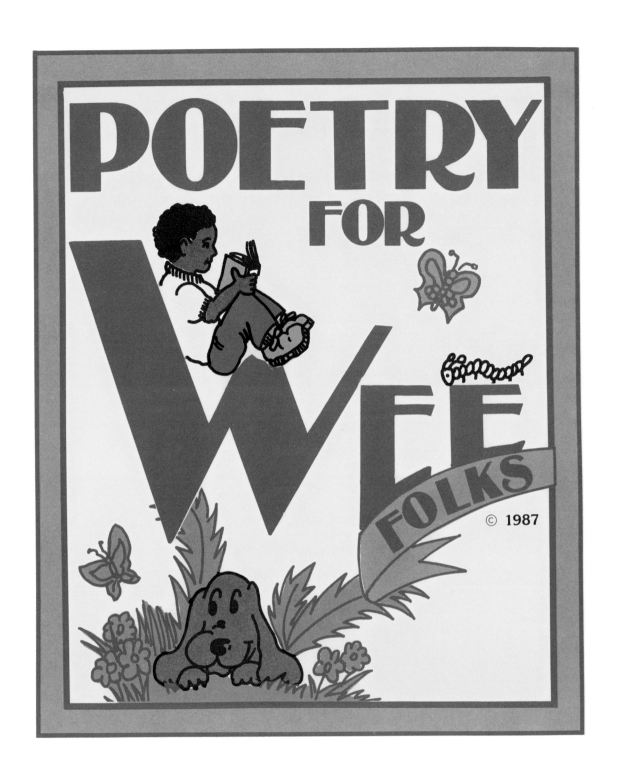

Written by Charlotte M. Hill

Illustrations by Sharon Jefferson and Theodore Fields

Elaine Annette Young-Art Director

Copyright 1987

Library of Congress Catalogue Card Number:
88-70281   ISBN 0-962-01820-1

Fourth Printing published by
Charill Publishers, St. Louis, Missouri
Printed in the United States of America

WEE FOLKS PLEDGE

My heritage is one of greatness;
And I know that I can do more.
I must never, never do less,
Than those who have gone before.

Dedicated to my four grandchildren who so often pull me happily into their wonderful world of play and make believe, the hundreds of primary children who have passed through the doors of my classroom for over twenty years and to ***God.***

TABLE OF CONTENTS

FEELINGS

Have you ever felt so angry,
That you thought you'd nearly pop?
Then a voice inside said softly,
Count to ten before you stop.

It's a trick my mother taught me,
Helps my anger go away.
And you know, it's really brought me
Better feelings for that day.

I've learned how to watch my temper,
I know how to think things through.
Now I see that it's much simpler,
If you try it you'll know too.

FEELING GOOD ABOUT ME

My folks seem to think that I
Am something really great.
They call me things like smart and sharp
On which I won't debate.

So I'll try to prove them right
Do what they expect of me.
I will work with all my might,
And be all that I can be.

That's why I feel good in knowing
They have confidence in me.
It makes me want to keep on growing
Just for all the world to see.

I CAN LEARN TO READ

I can learn to read, I know
Because my loved ones tell me so.
That's why I'll put my mind to work,
And never, never will I shirk.

I'll do my homework everyday;
It will be done before I play.
Then I can read the books I choose
And all this skill I'll never lose.

I'M LITERATE

Grown-ups who are literate,
Know how to read I'm told;
It's one of them that I intend to be.
Now here's the way I figure-it,
I'll read long before I'm old,
In fact, I'm reading now as you can see.

So I'll just keep on learning,
Getting better everyday;
For learning is the key to all success.
And when I'm all grown up, I'll say
My literacy has brought me happiness.

DON'T TALK TO STRANGERS

There's no such things as boogey-men
or goblins and such,
And I never cared for fairy tales too much.
The only boogey man a little kid like me
would meet,
Is the one you run into out on the street.

So don't talk to a stranger,
For he just might be a danger.
Keep your distance, run on home,
And remember, never, never, walk alone.

4

MY COLLECTION

I've got the neatest hiding place
For things I like to keep.
Some things I must put in a jar,
Lest from the drawer they'd leap.

There are grasshoppers, butterflies,
junebugs and snails,
Toy cars, flashlights, old rocks and nails.
Magnets, mirrors, sling-shots, and sticks,
You name it, I save it, until Mama kicks.

5

LOVE IS

Love is sharing with your brothers,
Love is doing right in school.
Love is being kind to others,
Trying not to break a rule.

Love is giving your respect,
To another human being.
It is doing what's correct,
Good in others always seeing.

Love will make your heart feel light,
Teach you not to pick a fight.
You will think on all things good,
Want to do the things you should.

THE MEANING OF GOOD MORNING

Good morning means so many things,
More things than I can name.
We say it for the joy it brings,
And gives out just the same.

It means I'm glad to see you,
Isn't it a lovely day.
It also means how do you do,
It's one more day to play,

Good morning simply means we care,
About all the folks we meet.
It means I'm glad that you are there,
To know and just to greet.

QUIET BOY

Shy little boy, how quiet you are,
We hardly know you are there.
You are so near and yet so far,
Do you think that we don't care?

Don't be frightened, little boy.
For we know that you are bright.
But you must speak out with joy,
When you know that you are right.

Since it's such a lovely day,
We can all go out to play.
We can romp out in the sun
And have lots and lots of fun.

MAMA CAME TO SCHOOL

Mama came to school one day,
To see how I was doing.
When I left home she didn't say,
This episode was brewing.

Now why'd she have to come just when,
I'd had a little trouble?
If teacher dared to tell her then,
I knew I'd get it double.

From now on I'll toe the line,
And things will turn out fine,
Since a kid can never know,
Just what day his mom will show.

CHRISTMAS VACATION

Every year at Christmas time,
Guess what we like to do?
Into the family car we climb,
With Grandma and Grandpa, too.

Daddy drives us through the city,
To see all the decorations,
Gee, I think it's such a pity,
That everyone's not on vacation.

The store windows are all lit up,
And everything looks so bright,
Even baby brother sits up,
To see the beautiful sights.

My heart sings the whole week through;
For the joy that Christmas brings,
And all the fun things that we do;
Oh, how my heart sings.

10

▌WISH

I wish that I could grow real tall,
And reach up to the sky,
then I would not be too small,
To walk on clouds up high.

I wish that I could be a star,
And twinkle all night long.
My light would shine so very strong,
You'd see me from afar.

I wish that I could make a wish,
For wishes never ending,
Then anytime within a swish,
I'd go on just pretending.

RECESS TIME

I'm happy when it's recess time
And we go out to play.
I'm gloomy when the sun won't shine,
For indoors we must stay.

Outside there's so much fun for me,
Like games and double-dutch,
What's more, I'm safe as I can be,
If I don't run too much.

When recess time is at an end,
We line up in the yard.
It's back to my own room again,
Where I'll work very hard.

MARTIN LUTHER KING, JR.

We had a lesson one day,
About Martin Luther King.
And I heard my teacher say,
Of his memory we must sing.

"Who was he?" asked my teacher,
And I said, "He was a preacher."
"Yes," she said, "He led the fights,
To help us gain our civil rights."

Martin never struck another,
His only weapon was his love.
He loved mankind as his brother,
Now he's gone to heaven above.

TELL THE TRUTH

Have you ever done something
That you never should have done,
And your mama never failed to ask you why?
Then you remember one thing,
That your daddy has said, "Son,
You must never, ever, ever tell a lie."

I try hard to mind my Dad,
Truthfulness can make me sad,
Especially when my little tricks,
Sometimes bring me painful licks.
Now I know that truth is best,
For it puts my mind at rest.

MAMA'S LITTLE HELPER

Sometimes when mama goes away,
I plan a nice surprise for her.
That day I don't go out to play,
I do things that are wiser.

I make my bed and dust the floor,
I tidy up the kitchen.
I wash the dishes and what's more,
I ask no one to pitch in.

It's fun to make my mom feel good,
Though I am only nine.
I do the things a smart kid should,
And now our house looks fine.

OLD BULLFROG

Funny old bullfrog,
Sitting on a log,
Looked up and saw me there.
Croak said bullfrog,
Yipes! I said,
He really gave me a scare.

Old bullfrog went hop, hop, hop,
And Zoom! he was out of sight.
I didn't dare say stop, stop, stop,
For he gave me such a fright.

MY TEACHER

I write love notes to my teacher,
Now let me tell you why.
There is no one who is neater,
For with her I don't feel shy.

She knows just when to praise me,
Reprimands me if I'm wrong.
From my sadness she can raise me,
And her patience is so long.

I like the way she teaches,
Tries to cause us little pain.
Even slower kids she reaches,
By explaining things again.

When the year-end comes I'll leave her,
Though I never want to go.
But I know I must believe her,
When she says that's how I'll grow.

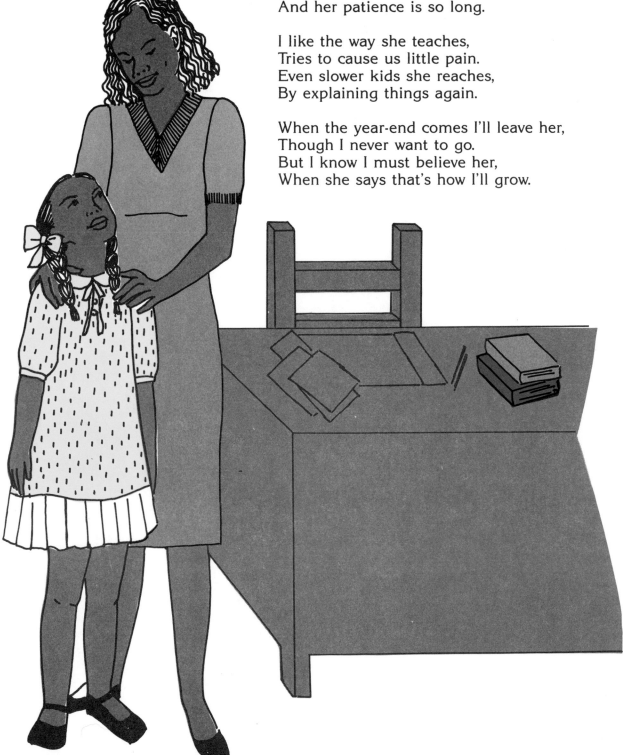

KIN FOLKS

Got a mama, a daddy, two grandmas,
Two aunts, an uncle, and two grandpas.
I'm the luckiest kid in town,
So many kin folks I'm never down.

Eat at one grandma's on Thanksgiving Day,
At Christmas the other can't keep me away.
Got lots of cousins that play with me,
And sisters and brothers well, I've got three.

It's so good having folks you love,
For love you can't have too much of.
I know that they all love me, too.
And folks like mine are very few.

MY LITTLE BROTHER

This may be hard for you to see,
But my brother did a funny thing.
One day he caught a bumblebee;
And on its leg he tied a string.

He didn't stop there, for goodness sake,
He caught a frog and even a snake.
Said he could teach the frog to talk.
And take the poor snake out for a walk.

But I'm still glad to have a kid brother,
And I wouldn't trade him for another.
Most times he acts pretty nice,
And sometimes listens to my advice.

GRANDFOLKS

When I was just a little tyke,
Before I started school,
I went to see my grandfolks every week.
Grandma fed me goodies and lots of sumptious food,
And grandpa gave me books that I could keep.

I'd turn the pages in my book as grandpa read to me,
And he never, ever really seemed to tire.
He'd let me sit for hours upon his loving knee,
And read and read to fill my heart's desire.

So if you want to learn good things
Like reading books and such,
Just go to see your grandfolks as I do.
No matter what you ask them, it never is too much,
And you will be as smart as I am, too.

MAMA'S GOODNIGHT KISS

Last night as I lay down to sleep,
I wasn't tired at all,
I thought that I'd try counting sheep,
And send them o'er the wall.

I counted and I counted,
And it came as no surprise,
That they mounted and they mounted,
Still I could not close my eyes.

Then Mama tip-toed to my bed,
Kissed me and tucked me in,
"Good night sweetheart," my Mama said,
And I never did reach ten.

MAKING UP

My friend and I fell out last week,
And for days we didn't speak.
Then yesterday she wanted to play,
Said soon she was moving away.

Now I really don't like to stay mad long,
Even if my friend is wrong,
Since we've had lots of fun in the past,
And I do want our friendship to last.

So if my friend moves far from us,
I'll miss her everyday,
But maybe I'll ride to her house by bus,
And again we'll be able to play.

MY DOG MIKEY

Mikey is my little pup,
That got out of the yard one day.
I searched and searched and nearly gave up,
For I thought he had run away.

I whistled and called all around the block,
I looked all around the house;
On my neighbors' doors I knocked and knocked,
But my Mikey I could not rouse.

Then just as it began to get dark
And I could no longer roam,
Suddenly, I heard a wonderful bark,
My Mikey had come back home!

PROPER ENGLISH

Learning proper English is often hard to do,
And I'm trying hard to learn to speak it right.
Some words we use with 'I' and 'you'
Another word with 'they',
Like 'am' and 'are' or 'have' and 'had'
Or 'is' and 'were' or 'was' and 'has',
Just be very careful what you say.

'Seen' needs the helping words,
Say 'have seen' without a doubt.
'Saw' needs no other verbs;
Watch and think on what comes out.
Learn to speak what is correct,
And then use it everyday.
Very soon I do suspect,
What you say will sound okay.

DUNE BOY

Dune Boy got to school today
at half past nine.
He looked at me, I looked at him,
And I knew that he'd been crying.
He slipped in the door,
Slid in his seat,
Took out his book and sniffed.
Poor Dune looked cross,
So I dared not speak,
Cause I knew we'd have a rift.

Sometimes we kids have days like that,
They just don't start out right.
If anybody even touched your hat,
They'd probably get a fight.
So I wait til later on that day,
And share my snacks with Dune.
Then he'll start laughing
and probably say,
Let's play again at noon.